All About
Magnets

by Stephen Krensky
illustrated by Paul Meisel

SCHOLASTIC INC.
New York Toronto London Auckland Sydney

For my father
– S.K.

With thanks to Dr. Anthony Ting, Stanford University,
for his assistance in preparing this book.

ISBN 0-590-45567-2

12 11 10 9 8 7 6 5 4 3 2 1   2 3 4 5 6 7/9

Printed in the U.S.A.   09

First Scholastic printing, October 1992

There is a story about a Greek shepherd named
Magnes who once lived about 2,500 years ago.
One day Magnes found a special stone.
This stone stuck to the iron tip of his
shepherd's crook.
Magnes knew the stone was unusual,
but he didn't do anything special with it.

Other such stones were later found.
And people began to wonder about them.
Maybe the stones were special, after all.
Maybe they were magical.

The stones could make iron dance, they said.
The stones could even make people fall in love.

But these stones were not really magical.
They were natural magnets.
A magnet is an object that contains metal
and attracts some other metals.
Natural magnets are found in rocks.
They have different shapes and sizes.

Magnets can be made by people, too.
There are bar magnets, horseshoe magnets,
and even magnets shaped like doughnuts.

DO IT YOURSELF

What Do Magnets Attract?

Remove the magnet from the back of this book.
Place the magnet on different objects.
Will your magnet zip a zipper?
Or pull a potato?
Can it attract buttons or crayons or paper bags?

Actually, magnets attract only some kinds of metal.
The most common is iron.
Test your magnet on coins, keys, and paper clips.
Your magnet will stick to the objects that
contain iron.
But it will not work on metals like brass, copper,
or aluminum.

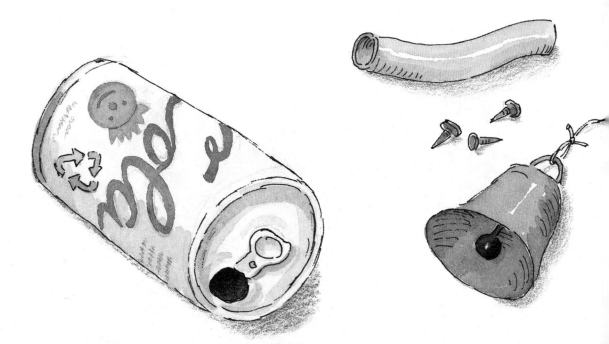

How does a magnet work?
Magnets are made of tiny pieces called molecules.
These molecules are much smaller than even
a speck of dust.
They are so small you can't see them with
your eyes alone.

In most objects, molecules are scattered
in different directions.
When molecules are scattered,
they are not magnetized.
They do not attract other objects.

In a magnet, all molecules face the same direction.
When molecules face the same direction,
they are magnetized.
They will attract some other metal objects.

These molecules are like rowers in a rowboat.
If they push or pull their oars in every direction,
the boat won't move.
But when the rowers face the same direction
and pull their oars at the same time,
the boat will move forward.
By working together the rowers use their
energy together.
The molecules in magnets work in a similar way.

Different-sized magnets have different strengths.
Even small magnets, though, can be very powerful.

DO IT YOURSELF

How Strong Is Your Magnet?

Put a paper clip on your magnet.
Hold just the magnet between two fingers.
Wave the magnet around.
Shake it up and down.
Can you make the paper clip fall off?
(It won't be easy!)

Magnets can also attract one thing through another.
The magnetic force passes through solid objects
the way light shines through glass.
And the stronger the magnet, the farther its force
can travel.

DO IT YOURSELF

Can Your Magnet Move Things Through Another Object?

Put a paper clip on top of a piece of paper.
Hold the paper flat with one hand.
Hold a magnet underneath it with your other hand.
Place the magnet under the paper clip.
Can you move the paper clip by moving the magnet?
Try the experiment again with construction paper
or cardboard instead of paper.
Does the paper clip still move through the thicker
materials?

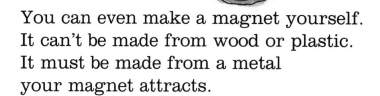

You can even make a magnet yourself.
It can't be made from wood or plastic.
It must be made from a metal
your magnet attracts.

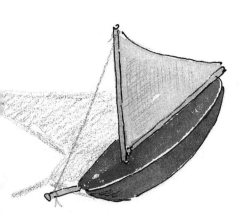

DO IT YOURSELF

Make Your Own Magnet

A paper clip can become a magnet.
Hold it lengthwise between your fingers.
With your other hand, rub the length of your
magnet along the paper clip.
You must rub the magnet in only one direction
on the paper clip (not back and forth).
Rub the magnet at least 50 times.
The paper clip is now weakly magnetized.
It will attract some metal objects.

Hold the end of the magnetized paper clip
against the end of another paper clip.
Do they stick together?

The two ends of every magnet are called poles.
One end is the north pole.
The other end is the south pole.
They both look the same.
But the magnetism at each end is different.
If you push two north poles toward each other,
they will repel each other and try to stay apart.
Two south poles will do the same thing.
However, the north pole of one magnet will attract
the south pole of another magnet.
The magnetic forces from the different poles
fit together like pieces in a jigsaw puzzle.

DO IT YOURSELF

Have a Magnet Race

On a piece of paper draw a starting line and
a finish line.
Put one magnet on the starting line.
Put a friend's magnet a little behind it.
Have your friend watch the clock.
Can you push your friend's magnet with your
magnet without having one touch the other?
(You must keep both north poles or both south
poles facing each other.)
How long does it take before your magnet
reaches the finish line?
Now let your friend try.
Whose magnet reached the finish line fastest?

The earth has a magnetic north and south pole, too.
They are close to the geographical North and
South poles.

The biggest magnet on earth is the earth itself.
The center of the earth, the inner core, is made
of metal.
It is mostly iron and nickel.
The outer core is made of molten rock.
This melted rock is so hot it flows like molasses.
It has metal in it, too.
The movement of the inner core against the outer
core has made the whole planet into a big magnet.
And like all magnets, it has magnetic north and
south poles.

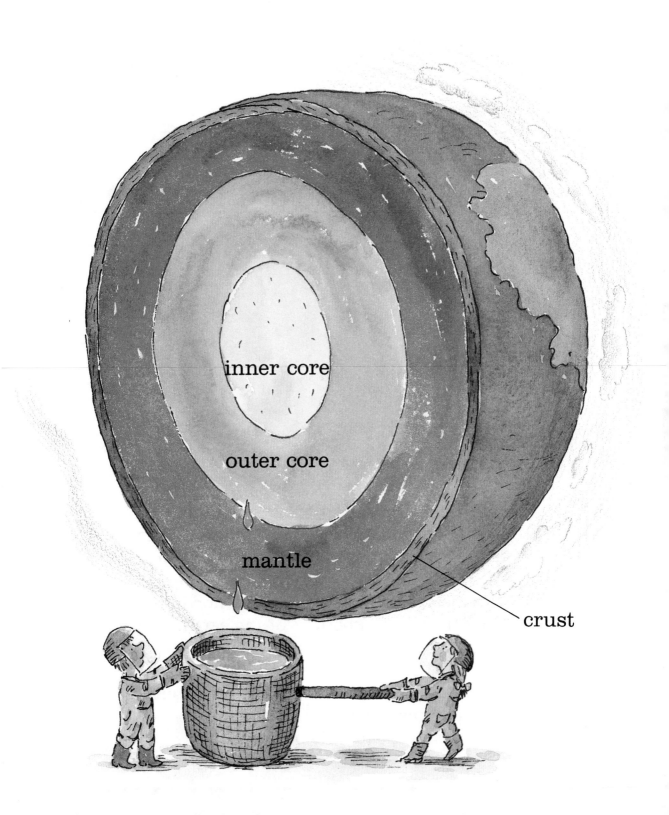

inner core

outer core

mantle

crust

The earth is very useful as a big magnet.
Almost a thousand years ago Chinese sailors
used a magnetized needle floating in water
to tell direction.
The needle always pointed along a north-south line
between the top and bottom of the earth.
It could feel the magnetic north and south poles
of the earth.
This invention kept track of the north-south
direction no matter where a person was.
It made a simple kind of compass.

DO IT YOURSELF

Make a Sailing Needle

Have an adult give you
an ordinary needle.
Carefully rub it with your magnet
at least 50 times.
(You may need some help.)
Remember to rub in only one direction.
When the needle is magnetized,
put it in a bowl of water.
Spin the needle around.
No matter how many times you spin it,
the needle will always point the same way,
along the magnetic north and south poles of the earth.

A few hundred years after the Chinese sailors
began using magnetic needles, Columbus
and other explorers used compasses
to help them cross the Atlantic Ocean.
Today compasses are still used at sea,
as well as places like forests or mountains,
where people can get lost without them.

Little magnets are useful as compasses,
but they can't lift or move anything big.
In 1820, Hans Oersted of Denmark discovered
that magnetism and electricity were related.
Oersted was a scientist who had experimented
with electricity for many years.

In his experiment, Oersted wrapped wire
around a steel rod.
When he sent electricity through the wire,
the rod became magnetized.

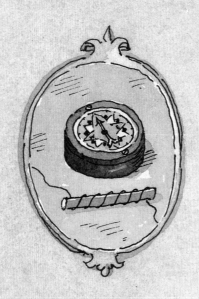

Oersted's discovery helped future scientists
develop powerful electromagnets by using
bigger rods and more electricity.

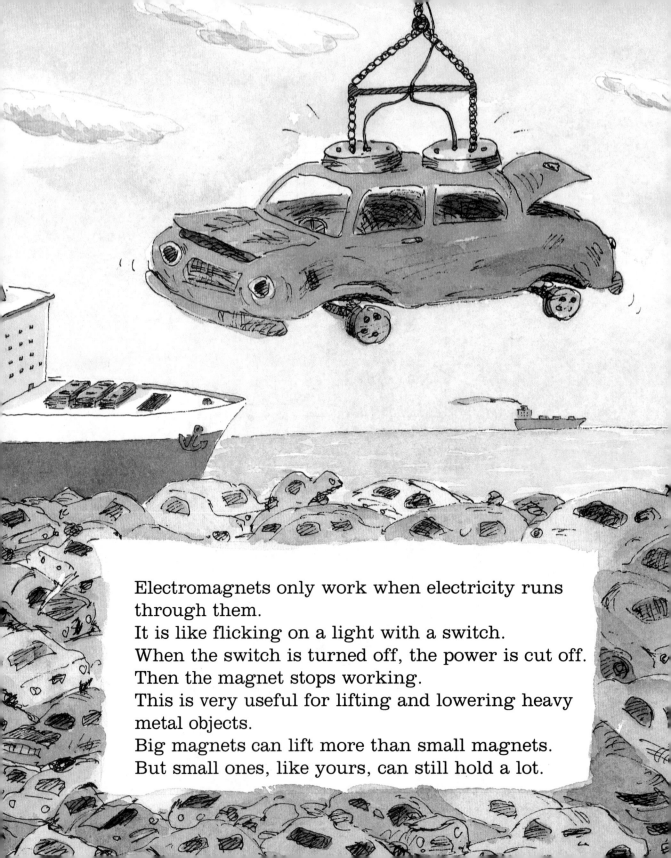

Electromagnets only work when electricity runs through them.
It is like flicking on a light with a switch.
When the switch is turned off, the power is cut off.
Then the magnet stops working.
This is very useful for lifting and lowering heavy metal objects.
Big magnets can lift more than small magnets.
But small ones, like yours, can still hold a lot.

DO IT YOURSELF

How Much Can Your Magnet Hold?

Hold your magnet in one hand.
Put one paper clip up against it.
Will the magnet hold the paper clip?
Now hook a second paper clip to the first.
Will the magnet hold them both?
Keep adding paper clips to the chain.
How many paper clips can your magnet lift?

Whether big or small, electromagnets are useful. Electromagnets of different sizes are found today in telephones, refrigerators, cars, and televisions.

If the Greek shepherd Magnes were living now,
he would be amazed by all the ways magnets
are used today.
They may not be magical stones, but they work
like magic in many parts of our daily life.

The LORAX

By
Dr. Seuss

HarperCollins *Children's Books*

For AUDREY, LARK *and* LEA
With Love

A CIP record for this title is available from the
British Library.
No part of this publication may be reproduced, stored
in a retrieval system or transmitted in any form or by
any means, electronic, mechanical, photocopying,
recording or otherwise, without the prior permission of
HarperCollins Publishers Ltd, 1 London Bridge Street
London SE1 9GF

37 39 40 38 36

ISBN: 978-0-00-717311-2

This edition published in the UK 2004 revised by
HarperCollins Children's Books 2009, a division of
HarperCollins Publishers Ltd, 1 London Bridge Street
London SE1 9GF

The HarperCollins website address is
www.harpercollins.co.uk

Printed and bound in Hong Kong

At the far end of town
where the Grickle-grass grows
and the wind smells slow-and-sour when it blows
and no birds ever sing excepting old crows...
is the Street of the Lifted Lorax.

And deep in the Grickle-grass, some people say,
if you look deep enough you can still see, today,
where the Lorax once stood
just as long as it could
before somebody lifted the Lorax away.

What *was* the Lorax?
And why was it there?
And why was it lifted and taken somewhere
from the far end of town where the Grickle-grass grows?
The old Once-ler still lives here.
Ask him. *He* knows.

You won't see the Once-ler.
Don't knock at his door.
He stays in his Lerkim on top of his store.
He lurks in his Lerkim, cold under the roof,
where he makes his own clothes
out of miff-muffered moof.
And on special dank midnights in August,
he peeks
out of the shutters
and sometimes he speaks
and tells how the Lorax was lifted away.

　　　　　　He'll tell you, perhaps...
　　　　　　if you're willing to pay.

On the end of a rope
he lets down a tin pail
and you have to toss in fifteen pence
and a nail
and the shell of a great-great-great-
grandfather snail.

Then he pulls up the pail,
makes a most careful count
to see if you've paid him
the proper amount.

Then he hides what you paid him
away in his Snuvv,
his secret strange hole
in his gruvvulous glove.

Then he grunts, "I will call you by Whisper-ma-Phone,
for the secrets I tell are for your ears alone."

SLUPP!
Down slupps the Whisper-ma-Phone to your ear
and the old Once-ler's whispers are not very clear,
since they have to come down
through a snergelly hose,
and he sounds
as if he had
smallish bees up his nose.

"Now I'll tell you,"he says, with his teeth sounding grey
"how the Lorax got lifted and taken away...

It all started way back...
such a long, long time back...

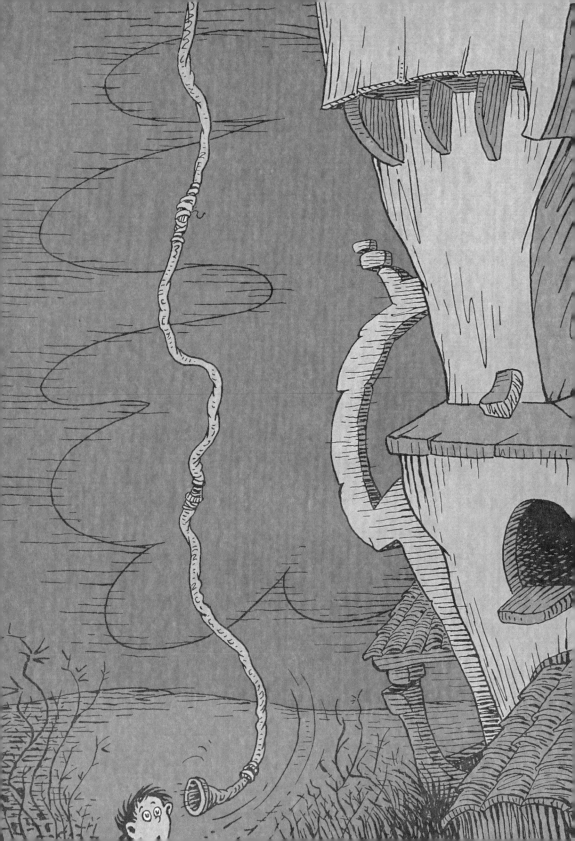

Way back in the days when the grass was still green
and the pond was still wet
and the clouds were still clean,
and the song of the Swomee-Swans rang out in space...
one morning, I came to this glorious place.
And I first saw the trees!
The Truffula Trees!
The bright-coloured tufts of the Truffula Trees!
Mile after mile in the fresh morning breeze.

ONCE-LER
WAGON

And, under the trees, I saw Brown Bar-ba-loots
frisking about in their Bar-ba-loot suits
as they played in the shade and ate Truffula Fruits.

From the rippulous pond
came the comfortable sound
of the Humming-Fish humming
while splashing around.

But those *trees!* Those *trees!*
Those Truffula Trees!
All my life I'd been searching
for trees such as these.
The touch of their tufts
was much softer than silk.
And they had the sweet smell
of fresh butterfly milk.

I felt a great leaping
of joy in my heart.
I knew just what I'd do!
I unloaded my cart.

In no time at all, I had built a small shop.
Then I chopped down a Truffula Tree with one chop.
And with great skilful skill and with great speedy speed,
I took the soft tuft. And I knitted a Thneed!

The instant I'd finished, I heard a *ga-Zump!*
I looked.
I saw something pop out of the stump
of the tree I'd chopped down. It was sort of a man.
Describe him?... That's hard. I don't know if I can.

He was shortish. And oldish.
And brownish. And mossy.
And he spoke with a voice
that was sharpish and bossy.

"Mister!" he said with a sawdusty sneeze,
"I am the Lorax. I speak for the trees.
I speak for the trees, for the trees have no tongues.
And I'm asking you, sir, at the top of my lungs"—
he was very upset as he shouted and puffed—
"*What's that THING you've made out of my Truffula tuft?*"

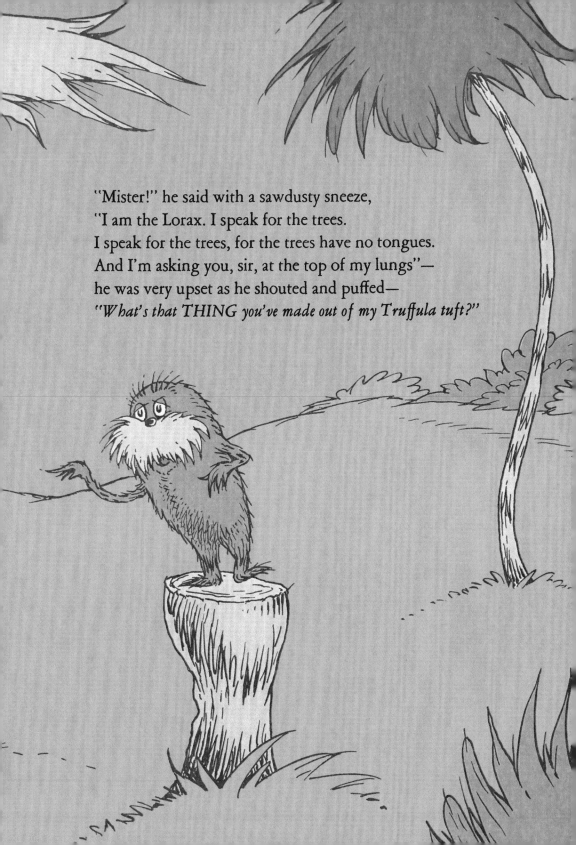

"Look, Lorax," I said. "There's no cause for alarm.
I chopped just one tree. I am doing no harm.
I'm being quite useful. This thing is a Thneed.
A Thneed's a Fine-Something-That-All-People-Need!
It's a shirt. It's a sock. It's a glove. It's a hat.
But it has *other* uses. Yes, far beyond that.
You can use it for carpets. For pillows! For sheets!
Or curtains! Or covers for bicycle seats!"

The Lorax said,
"Sir! You are crazy with greed.
There is no one on earth
who would buy that fool Thneed!"

But the very next minute I proved he was wrong.
For, just at that minute, a chap came along,
and he thought that the Thneed I had knitted was great.
He happily bought it for three ninety-eight.

I laughed at the Lorax, "You poor stupid guy!
You never can tell what some people will buy."

"I repeat," cried the Lorax,
"I speak for the trees!"

"I'm busy," I told him.
"Shut up, if you please."

I rushed 'cross the room, and in no time at all,
built a radio-phone. I put in a quick call.
I called all my brothers and uncles and aunts
and I said, "Listen here! Here's a wonderful chance
for the whole Once-ler Family to get mighty rich!
Get over here fast! Take the road to North Nitch.
Turn left at Weehawken. Sharp right at South Stitch."

And, in no time at all,
in the factory I built,
the whole Once-ler Family
was working full tilt.
We were all knitting Thneeds
just as busy as bees,
to the sound of the chopping
of Truffula Trees.

Then...
Oh! Baby! Oh!
How my business did grow!
Now, chopping one tree
at a time
was too slow.

So I quickly invented my Super-Axe-Hacker
which whacked off four Truffula Trees at one smacker.
We were making Thneeds
four times as fast as before!
And that Lorax?...
He didn't show up any more.

But the next week
he knocked
on my new office door.

He snapped, "I'm the Lorax who speaks for the trees
which you seem to be chopping as fast as you please.
But I'm *also* in charge of the Brown Bar-ba-loots
who played in the shade in their Bar-ba-loot suits
and happily lived, eating Truffula Fruits.

"NOW...thanks to your hacking my trees to the ground,
there's not enough Truffula Fruit to go 'round.
And my poor Bar-ba-loots are all getting the crummies
because they have gas, and no food, in their tummies!

"They loved living here. But I can't let them stay.
They'll have to find food. And I hope that they may.
Good luck, boys," he cried. And he sent them away.

I, the Once-ler, felt sad
as I watched them all go.
BUT…
business is business!
And business must grow
regardless of crummies in tummies, you know.

I meant no harm. I most truly did not.
But I had to grow bigger. So bigger I got.
I biggered my factory. I biggered my roads.
I biggered my wagons. I biggered the loads
of the Thneeds I shipped out. I was shipping them forth
to the South! To the East! To the West! To the North!
I went right on biggering...selling more Thneeds.
And I biggered my money, which everyone needs.

Then *again* he came back! I was fixing some pipes
when that old-nuisance Lorax came back with *more* gripes.

"I am the Lorax," he coughed and he whiffed.
He sneezed and he snuffled. He snarggled. He sniffed.
"Once-ler!" he cried with a cruffulous croak.
"Once-ler! You're making such smogulous smoke!
My poor Swomee-Swans...why, they can't sing a note!
No one can sing who has smog in his throat.

"And so," said the Lorax,
"—please pardon my cough—
they cannot live here.
So I'm sending them off.

"Where will they go?...
I don't hopefully know.

They may have to fly for a month...or a year...
To escape from the smog you've smogged-up around here.

"What's *more*," snapped the Lorax. (His dander was up.)
"Let me say a few words about Gluppity-Glupp.
Your machinery chugs on, day and night without stop
making Gluppity-Glupp. Also Schloppity-Schlopp.
And what do you do with this leftover goo?...
I'll show you. You dirty old Once-ler man, you!

"You're glumping the pond where the Humming-Fish hummed!
No more can they hum, for their gills are all gummed.
So I'm sending them off. Oh, their future is dreary.
They'll walk on their fins and get woefully weary
in search of some water that isn't so smeary.
I hear things are just as bad up in Lake Erie."

THNEEDS

And then I got mad.
I got terribly mad.
I yelled at the Lorax, "Now listen here, Dad!
All you do is yap-yap and say, 'Bad! Bad! Bad! Bad!'
Well, I have my rights, sir, and I'm telling *you*
I intend to go on doing just what I do!
And, for your information, you Lorax, I'm figgering
on biggering

and BIGGERING

and BIGGERING

and BIGGERING,

turning MORE Truffula Trees into Thneeds
which everyone, EVERYONE, *EVERYONE* needs!"

And at that very moment, we heard a loud whack!
From outside in the fields came a sickening smack
of an axe on a tree. Then we heard the tree fall.
The very last Truffula Tree of them all!

No more trees. No more Thneeds. No more work to be done.
So, in no time, my uncles and aunts, every one,
all waved me good-bye. They jumped into my cars
and drove away under the smoke-smuggered stars.

Now all that was left 'neath the bad-smelling sky
was my big empty factory…
the Lorax…
and I.

The Lorax said nothing. Just gave me a glance...
just gave me a very sad, sad backward glance...
as he lifted himself by the seat of his pants.
And I'll never forget the grim look on his face
when he heisted himself and took leave of this place,
through a hole in the smog, without leaving a trace.

And all that the Lorax left here in this mess
was a small pile of rocks, with the one word . . .
"UNLESS."
Whatever *that* meant, well, I just couldn't guess.

That was long, long ago.
But each day since that day
I've sat here and worried
and worried away.
Through the years, while my buildings
have fallen apart,
I've worried about it
with all of my heart.

"But *now*," says the Once-ler, .
"Now that *you're* here,
the word of the Lorax seems perfectly clear.
UNLESS someone like you
cares a whole awful lot,
nothing is going to get better.
It's not.

"SO...
Catch!" calls the Once-ler.
He lets something fall.
"It's a Truffula Seed.
It's the last one of all!
You're in charge of the last of the Truffula Seeds.
And Truffula Trees are what everyone needs.
Plant a new Truffula. Treat it with care.
Give it clean water. And feed it fresh air.
Grow a forest. Protect it from axes that hack.
Then the Lorax
and all of his friends
may come back."